CRYSTAL POETRY

CRYSTAL
POETRY

adela GIBSON

ISBN:
978-621-434-082-8 (softcover)
978-621-434-083-5 (hardcover)
978-621-434-084-2 (eBook)

Printed in New York by:

OMNIBOOK CO.
99 Wall Street, Suite 118
New York, NY 10005
USA
+1 202-738-1322
www.omnibookcompany.com

First Edition

For e-book purchase: Kindle on Amazon, Barnes and Noble
Book purchase: Amazon.com, Barnes & Noble, and
www.omnibookcompany.com
Omnibook titles may be purchased in bulk for educational, business, fund-raising, or sales promotional use. For more information please e-mail **info@omnibookcompany.com**

Cover design by: Gian Carlo Tan

CONTENTS

YOUR ONE AND ONLY LADY

When I smiled at you, I could tell you were my kind of guy
Wasn't what you said, just the way you looked into my eye
I really didn't want to go but I truly could not stay
Let me tell you boy, you're the one that makes me feel this way

Let me just say this, we can seal it with a kiss
Let me be your baby – Your one and only lady

Don't make me cry, I just want you to be my guy
Let me be your baby - Your one and only lady

I want to share your world and be your only girl
Let me be your baby - Your one and only lady

And OOO! -When I saw your smile, OOO! – It made my heartbeat wild
I could feel the heat – Boy! - You really rocked my style
I really didn't want to go but I truly could not stay
I love you so much and I want to be with you each day

Wait a minute! Hold up! – Just let me tell it one more time
Do you feel what I'm saying - I need you to be all mine.

Can I say it again; want to be more than a friend
I want to be your baby – Your one and only lady

Don't make me cry, I want you to be my guy
Let me be your baby - Your one and only lady

I want to share your world and be your only girl
Just let me be your baby - Your one and only lady

UNCLE JIM

His face was full of the earth's red clay and its buried gold
Sus manos eran fuerte y precisos con el hatchet he would hold

He'd chop the stalks of cane then to the ground they would fall
El haria pivotar muy fuerte y rapido one swing was all

He'd gather them up until they completely filled the crocosac
Luego volveria a caminar into the shed carrying them on his back

He would save some for guests, but the best would always be mine
A veces iba ser tranquilo, pero para mi siempre fue sweet and kind

Mi heroe enviado del Dios era alto muy smart and slim
My protective shield and mentor was found in my Uncle Jim

Cuando estaba triste o enfermo, there's nada he did not do
Para me, the bottom line is this is plain and simply true

No se porque tomo tanto tiempo para escribir about him
One thing I can tell you is siempre me ha gustado mi Uncle Jim.

THIS MAN, MY BROTHER

A shy, quiet, yet fun and honest man
Going through this life as only he can
All his intricacies I cannot tell
There's a part of him I don't know so well

The things I that have learned of him, for sure
In this poem for him I will procure
Forgive me please, if you don't think I'm right
I can only sketch from my own eyesight

This man of life, this man is my brother
Possessing a style unlike none other
Certainly, talent is a part of him
Sharing with us his own special rhythm

Right out of Webster's, his words seem to flow
He says his genius is quite apropos
He smiles while he says yep yep, duckplucker!
Now tell me have you met such a brother

Knowing this man for me is a pleasure
His friendship is one I truly treasure
This man, my friend, this man is my brother
He's one of a kind, there is none other

ELUSIVE LOVE

I come to find out from you once again
Is there hope for us or just an amen
Why do you question all I do and say
Why can't you put a little trust my way
I've known you now for a very long time
You speak of roses; you reminisce of wine
What more is there for us
If not the world, then heaven above
What more is there for us
But only to taste the elusive love
Why do ignore what you truly feel
Give in to your heart; you know that it's real
You look at me with passion in your eyes
But hide your love behind some grim disguise
I'm afraid that our time has passed us by
And I weep, though it does no good to cry
What more is there for us
If not the world, then heaven above
What more is there for us
But only to taste the elusive love.

BROWN EYES

Your brows arch boldly, yet ever so lightly over
Your big beautiful deep brown eyes

Those beautiful caramel brown love eyes
Poetry can only give hint of their beauty

And touch upon the loveliness of your dimples
That eternally kisses the corners of your mouth

Your nose curves sharply pointing to
Your lips that curl into peppermint smiles

Your cheeks that give high praises to your face
Gently caressing all as if between loving hands

Your skin of golden honey flows harmoniously
Over and around those big brown eyes

They reflect all I see in you and I reflect it back
In this poem of you and your beautiful brown eyes

THE SPIRIT OF TIME

Certainly, you know, I know, we all know
That to the winds this life must blow

We cannot runaway; we cannot hide
For on vestige elements our essence ride

Without our frames, we still can climb
Truly running to, but not from Time

There's no escape – No! Nowhere to run
It will do no good when finally Time has come

We can go to a planet or dream on a star
Time will find us no matter where we are

The winds in our favor will not bow down
The earth for us will echo no sound

No! Don't be afraid – there's no need to cry
For Time will be there even when we die

In the farthest corners and darkest spaces
Times voice will fill the emptiest places

Surely, you know, I know, we all know
That running from Time, leaves nowhere to go

Don't think you've escaped or have gotten away
For Time is always there with each new day

Time is here, present, future and past
Time was here first and Time will be last!

MATURITY

Growing up is
Exchanging baby dolls
For a real one
And mama for a man

Dressing up is
Putting on a smile
Instead of a frown
And airs for clothes

Finding out is
Seeing your dreams
Turn into realities
While trust fade into lies

Having fun is
Using the games
To get over
While being a loser

Maturity is
Locking up the
Spirit inside of you
And dying each time you do

NO FRIEND OF MINE

Once I believed you were truly my friend
That false train of thought is now at an end
You took the only one who warmed my soul
Leaving me alone and out in the cold

You said that you wished the best for me
And hoped that happy I would always be
Into empty space all your words must fly
For now I see that they were all a lie

A friend wouldn't take the true love I had
And honestly think I wouldn't feel bad
You took my lover, my true ecstasy
You took everything away from me

You played foul and nasty game on me
Did you really think that I would not see
That you are most sadly the biggest fool
Because no friend of mine would be so cruel

THE BOTTOM LINE

How can you say
I've got to hold on to
What I've got baby!

What about us
We don't have anything
Really worth having

We have nothing
Aside from each other
Now that is a good time

But, Love is not always
Good times, it 's rough times too
And that's the Bottom Line

NUBIAN LOVE

Nubian being in the garden of my love
Setting free the dormant spirit inside us
Singing a Nubian love song inside my ear
Causing the Euphrates to flow through me

We played at the pyramids along the Giza
We prayed at temples that were in Songhai
And danced to the beat of ancestral drums
Giving praises for the Majestic Nile

The God family has blessed our union
That we may remain in love together
As we explore from Ethiopia to Ghana
Two sparks of African love: United

Nubian sentry in the garden of our love
Setting free the true spirit inside of us
Singing an African love song in my ear
Causing the Zambezi to flow through me

HERE WE GO AGAIN

Here we go again in the same old rut
With the same old song instilled in our gut
Here we go again doing things the same old way
We have the same old thoughts that don't decay

Here we go again watching the world go by
As we hear the songs of hungry children cry
The good and the bad, they all share our street
Trains and buses are filled with the clatter of feet

Here we go again with the old refrain
Seems we spend so much of our lives in vain
We play that same old game – the one called sin
While stealing dreams from a bottle of gin

We cheat the Lord
Then we say Amen
But I still say
Here we go again!

MY LOVE FOR YOU

My love for you is greater than
The stars, the sun, the moon
My love for you is not too late
Nor does it come too soon

A sunny breeze, a flower's scent
So gentle and so meek
My love for you brings humbly
The answers that you seek

My love for you will never end
Nor will it ever change
My love for you reaches farther than
The heaven's open range

HEART TO HEART

Love, what is it that I've done to you
That makes you stay far away from me
My contemplation has lent no clue
To anything that you would fancy

Our shared moments they are less than few
Not for lack of opportunity
Though many times you have missed your cue
Neglecting to turn the special key

Love what is it that I have to do
To help you so that soon you may see
That your evasiveness has been undue
Thus I await your apology

Just let me have a small peek-a-boo
I won't hurt – you can rely on me
I'd like to be a part of your crew
Tell me what is the admission fee

Love, for me, you are certainly new
I always thought that you would be free
Now I have a somewhat different view
You are such a rare commodity

HANDS

The hands that held mine
Just didn't know
That within their palms
I had placed my woe

All the tears I cried
Into these hands did flow
So my gratitude goes to
The hands that made me glow

The hands upon which now
A kiss goodbye I must bestow
The hands I needed yesterday
Today, I must let go

DID YOU EVER?

Did you ever reach out for a love that wasn't there?
Did you ever try to touch and all you felt was air?
Did you ever get that feeling that made you want to die?
Did you ever feel, no matter what, you have got to try?
Did you ever think about life and what it means to you?
Did you ever hope that someday, your dreams will come true?
Did you ever feel that you have got to get away?
Did you ever pray that soon, you'll see a brighter day?
Did you ever dream you had everything you ever wanted?
Did you ever feel somehow you were being haunted?
Did you ever feel strange, like you really don't belong?
Did you ever feel weak, but pretended to be strong?
Did you ever feel the need for a love that wasn't there?
Did you ever try to touch but thought no one would care?

MAGIC MAN

He dabbed honey on my lips, for me, to taste
Then took it back and let it go to waste
I watched as the golden drops fell to the floor
And wondered why I couldn't have any more
He teemed my days with love's sweet musk
Then the magic man turned dawn into dusk
I saw love's stardust blowing away
And dared to wish some for another day
What the magic man did, I call it treason
He turned away without warning or reason
He waved his hand like a wand of magic
And made today defy yesterday's logic
I heard my poor heart sob tears of grief
I pleaded with him to start a new leaf
But the magic man only looks while I cry
He hasn't enough magic to make my tears dry

NO DEAD END STREET

We are no dead end street
We are chock full of endless voltage
Brimming with ideas not yet thought
And desires not yet dreamed
Our mind is a mosaic of imagery
A never-ending scene of excitement
That splashes out colors that have no name
And forming words that have not been heard
For we are all inventors that haven't invented
We are the genies without recognition, but
We are no dead end street

Each of us is a design; a work of art
Like snowflakes all beautiful, but none the same
Our purpose is to share our joy
To tickle the mind with a new tingle
To embrace a thought of a new texture
That can now be the essence of what has been
So that if we meet, greet and then part
We can learn each other's tints and hues
So that we may engage the creative forces that we are
Then can state with surety and without doubt that
We are no dead end street

ECSTASY

When you speak, you speak my silent dreams
When we kiss, sweet nectars flow inside your mouth
When we touch,I feel your true self touching me
I feel the pain of pleasure that is called ecstasy

I see your zest for life blazing in the sun
I see your smile projecting, shining in the moon
I see the god within you coming into me
I hear the voice of passion that we call ecstasy

Though you are a dream, I know that you are real
Though I've known you sparsely, I've known you forever
Though I cannot define what is happening to me
I know within myself and yours, that this is ecstasy

MIDNIGHT FLOWERS

Once ago they bloomed
Full wild and untamed
There were so many then
Yet none had earned its fame
They no longer spread pretty
Designs up toward the sun
They've begun to fade away
Each petal – one by one
All that remains is Hope
The beginning of all things
Like butterflies
Waiting to borne new wings
And spread their joy across
Some eager untouched land
And nurture their seedlings
According to the Master's plan

THE WEDDING VOW

Let the sweet love which we possess
Be the cause of our eternal happiness
Let the gladness the fills our hearts
Be in the end as it was from the start

Let the smile that lights up my face
Be filled with joy when we embrace
Let the pride the swells our soul
Be the pride that never grows old

Let all the beauty that we see
Remind me of you and you of me
Let the star twinkling in our eyes
Grow endlessly bright and never dies

Let the music which fills our ears
Play for us through all our years
Now we are one – no longer two
Our love will last 'til time is through

GENESIS

Take a little fire
Roll it into a ball
Add some feeling to it
Then give it all your all

Hurl it long and hard
Into the black of night
Let it explode
Into a blinding light

Watch it floating gently
It will gently subside
But the light will shine on
And forever live inside

NATURE'S FORCE

The sky winks, another day passes by
Another day without you to talk to
And without me there to ask you "why"
The wink is another evening to satisfy

The wind whispers that you're waiting for me
Waiting for that special bloom from inside
To tell me here is where you ought to be
It whispers: Vous est dans mon coeur ma cherie

The sun smiles a feeling beyond any measure
A feeling that only we can share
It's a veil of ultimate pleasure
That gives us life's true and greatest treasure

LESSON IN FUTILITY

Nonchalant attitudes lends no credibility or substance to this partnership

However, we do what matters for those who matters most to the both of us

We have been pushing and sometimes pulling this load of non-intimacies

Up a very long and steep hill hoping to get to higher, more level grounds

Putting up with unloving, chronic abusiveness that we call a relationship

My shoulders had grown weary and I couldn't hold it so I had to let it go

It crashed so hard and when I turned around to look at you I realized that

The struggle was mine and mine alone and all you could say was: "Sorry"

No repeat players here, it's a sticky situation where mostly precious time is lost.

Game over, losers leave no better than when they came; there are no winners here.

SEPTEMBER'S BLUE

The sadness we've felt for so long
Is wrapped so simply in your song
We know that you're with us always
You have been right here all along

We will do whatever it takes
Because in life there are no breaks
We keep precious our memories
Giving us strength that never shakes

Keeping it real and staying true
Full of love is September's Blue
Keeping it real, seeing it through
There's magic in September's Blue

Love is transcending time and space
Filling our hearts with peace and grace
It makes us sure that soon in time
We will meet again face to face

We drink deep from our loving cup
Knowing we must never give up!
Lifting our glasses way up high
In praise before festive joys erupt

Keeping it real and staying true
Full of love is September's Blue
Keeping it real, seeing it through
Magic is there in September's Blue

TIME TO SAY "WHEN"

The elders have always said to the sojourner
Live your life and have fun to the bitter end
Hold on tight to love, friends and laughter
When it stops is when you have to say "when"

When you know what you bring to the table
Are unwanted and underappreciated goods
When the words you speak falls on deaf ears
And ends up with the "misunderstoods"

When all that you have struggled hard for
Adds up to a pitifully high heap of naught
It's clear this is a battle that has been lost
There's no good reason it was ever fought

When you can no longer be relaxed and
Where you are is not what you call home
Then it's time to say "when" and let it go
Give it to God and bid them all shalom!

TODAY, TOMORROW, FOREVER

Your love runs so deep and fills me up sweetly
Your spirit is strong, loving me completely

I've missed you more than you could ever know
Remembering our special magic makes me glow

Yesterday we missed our special time together
Today love is ours; tomorrow it's forever

Your words still linger deep in me for an eternity
No one will ever make me doubt your sincerity

Those who are against us can no longer hide
They must let go and get off that hater's ride

Yesterday we missed our special time together
Today love is ours; tomorrow it's forever

We are now in control - we are now in command
We have the victory and finally united we stand

We missed yesterday when we couldn't be together
Today love is ours; tomorrow it will be forever

MEMORIES

I remember when you would call me "baby"
And whisper sweet things in my ear
I remember hearing love within your soul
When you'd say "lover, come here"
I remember how I use to call you
Just to tell you that I really cared
Yes I remember everything about you
And all the moments that we have shared
I remember when I needed you
You came, you were always there
I remember holding you in my arms
And being happy because you were near
All the times we'd spent together
How could I forget them, any one
For all the rough times we'd been through
There always was a shining ray of sun.
Even when there was no longer a "me and you"
We still reminisced of when you were mine
All the memories, yes, they are good
And will always float endless in time.

TERMINAL

Can't deal with this tattered and weak connection,
Now a nightmare episode of a much too long trip
Depicting what you call a long-term relationship.
Don't like this too shaky and very rocky slope
All the while we were looking for some solid ground
All I want is to take a load off; find a spot to sit down

REFRAIN:
This is what I call terminal
It's truly criminal
Not the way it should be
Not what I want from you; for me

I didn't know until it crashed until I had to let it go!
I realized the struggle was all mine and mine alone
It hurt throughout my soul all the way down to my bone
I'm stretched to the core there's no more for you and me
When you leave be sure to take your "sorries" with you
And please don't forget to take your empty words too

MY FAVORITE TEACHER

My favorite teacher is sweet and black
She taught me how to seek out all the facts
I was lucky to have her in fourth grade
So I could witness the wonders she made
I remember what she had tried to explain
That life was joyful but there's also pain
She said, children, take the good with the bad
Learn to enjoy the bitter with the sweet
Yet she never lost her beautiful beat
She loved being black before it was famed
Soon we met the hardships she had named
Sometimes she'd talk until our ears would swell
Now I'm glad she did; now I wish her well
She was so much more than just a teacher
More like a mother; sometimes a preacher
We need her in our community
Helping the little children just like me

LIVING INSIDE OUR SONG

Ever since we danced together
I've been living inside our song
Dancing it with someone else
Just feels and seems all wrong
I remember how you held me
So tightly as we danced
Mind, body and spirit
All at once romanced
It was the first we danced
And probably it was the last
The song was for our future
But we danced it in the past
Because we are not together
And I'm one lonely girl
Now all I have is this song
And I've made this song my world

TO MY PEOPLE

I don't want to hear no more talk of oppression
We have gladly accepted too many concessions
We have got to trust and love one another
You are my Sister, You are my Brother!

We have lived too many years of atrocities
How much more will it take before you see
You need to love you; therefore loving me
So we can see the truth, which will make us free!

No more pulling the knives out our back
Because some of us want to be on the attack
Let the Willie Lynch letter become a lie
Let our self destruction and it's hatred die!

Then no one across any of God's land
Will be able to take us away from The Plan
And make us think that we don't belong
And make us feel that we are not strong!

We have to believe and know who we are
We are the builders of ships that visit afar
We performed intricate surgeries long ago
We built many pyramids, I'm sure you know!

It is not a part of our ancestral heritage to fight
My people, it is past the time, we need to unite
It will take some time since we've lost our way
But once we get started it will be child's play!

My people, we have got to live in unity
It is the only way that we can be free
We must go back to find our spirituality
So we can appreciate our individuality!

TO THINK OF YOU

To think of you is as lovely as a rhyme
For if the stars should all fade away tonight
We would still have the joy of love in our time
And if we should happen upon heaven's light
It would draw us closer to the ties that bind
Just you and I sailing our love in the night
Just us two guiding a love that's yours and mine

To think of you is enchantment to my mind
A romantic evening with soft candlelight
And silver goblets filled with our favorite wine
As we toast our passion this and every night
While the music plays on sweetly as we dine
Just us two, not letting love out of our sight
Just you and I in a love that's yours and mine

To think of you always make me feel so fine
I want the world to see that our love is bright
And to never doubt its blessings for mankind
Is magnified by the power of its might
So that all those who seek may be sure to find
Just you and I holding our love very tight
Just us two living a love that's yours and mine

LADY WINTER

Winter is a jealous lady
Who loves to know she's missed
She seems to want us to forget
That springtime ever did exist

She nestles all her children
Keeping them all indoors
As she cools off the earth
And tends her other chores

When all her work is done
Her children can come out and play
For she is weary now
And must give up her stay

She kisses us good-bye
And bids us all adieu
Then says "Take care children
See you when autumn is through

ATTRACTION

I cannot quite understand
Why I am so attracted to this man
I sometimes look up into the sky
Wishing the stars would tell me why

It seems as if I can't control
The sensations pulsating through my soul
I often feel your presence near
But when I look, there's nil but air

Yet I am sure deep down inside of me
That I can find you where eyes cannot see
I am positive that with time
A place in this reality, we will find

I know that you are aware
Of mutual feelings that we both share
You seem to have strong hold the key
To something locked inside of me

Somehow I've got to find out what is it
That makes confidence counterfeit
I'm curious to know and ready to learn
What makes the fire in your eyes burn

What is it that you want of me
The future holds lesson for me to see
The thing I need most to understand
Is why am I so attracted to this man

Fantasy

I live in a world of pure fantasy
It helps me deal with this reality
Life's not what I expected it to be
Fantasy is much easier for me

I live in a world of pure fantasy
Dreaming up visions of pure ecstasy
This world has been tougher than it should be
Fantasy is a lovely place to be

I live in a world of pure fantasy
It's the only place where I can be free
Everything else tries to put chains on me
At least fantasy holds no misery

I live in a world of pure fantasy
There no one can make a fool out of me
There I am as happy as I can be
There I can be with whom I want to be

I live in a world of pure fantasy
It helps me deal better with reality
Because love has long since forgotten me
And fantasy is all that's left for me

O. N. & A.

I am O.
I am mentally able and strong
I take life by the horn
I steer it where I want to go
I am O.

I am N.
I am smart and spiritual
I will do whatever it takes
I will surely make it happen
I am N.

I am A.
I am filled with humor
I can make the world smile
I am doing it in my own way
I am A.

SONNY

Wynter was warm and bright when you were here
Watching football while Mom was of full of cheer

You'd always talk about going to school
Cousin, you made it sound like it was cool

I guess that's why you ended up teaching
To all the young minds that you were reaching

That summer you drove down the rocky side
That summer, sadly, would be your last ride

I never got a chance to say adieu
Nor the chance to say, Sonny, I love you

LOVERS CIRCLE

With the deepness of love I pen this line
I adored your spirit and you did mine
So smooth, so bold, rich like the finest wine
Drunk with fullness of our similar rhyme
Dipped in the magic of its own sweet time
A greater love than Lord Tennyson's line
The strongest ever, no doubt, God's design
It stays true even as we close this line

TEST

I have enjoyed the sunshine of each new day
I've tried hard to find a better and easier way
I have gone back in order to find a new design
Looking for that extra special one of a kind
Each time I got close enough to try to rest
I 'd be out again taking the same old test
I realize there were lessons I needed to learn
A whole new world whose trails I had to burn
For what it's worth there were things I had to try
But also things I had to do before I say goodbye

The Lyricist

The vantage point: a significant time or a particular place
Cultivated for emphasis or put to music so you can keep the pace
Watch the ripple effects as simple and gentle as a flowing tear
Which can change the mood or tone and quickly turn into fear
The words will create music as it plucks a string in the heart
It is a jam session for the soul, mind and our spiritual eye
It answers the question before we can ask the inevitable "why?"
The vantage point of things past or present, good or bad
Can be a joy that has been confused with that which is sad
Meanwhile rekindling fires that have laid dormant far too long
Which now burn with raging energy that is vibrant and strong

SPRING FEVER

I met him one day and the world ceased to spin
Looked in his eyes and knew this could be no sin
We fussed and we cussed, as lovers often do
But I made up my mind that our love was true

In the park, we played ring around the rosy
All the while our love was becoming dozy
It couldn't be love; it must be spring fever you see
If it were truly love he would still be here with me

I left him with tears streaming inside my heart
That was when the heartbreak had chosen to start
I would search the sky for silence then I'd pray
Dearest Lord, why did he have to go away

I miss him and really don't want any other
If he'd come back he'd have love like no other
It couldn't be love; it must be spring fever you see
If it were truly love he would still be here with me

MY BALL

My ball is so big, round and green
My ball can be so cruel and mean
My big ball is infested with lies and sin
The match-up with hell, it's goal to win
It is ourselves that we've been harming
What we've done has caused global warming
My ball is kept so dull and murky
I don't think that we are really worthy
My ball is brightest at high noon
And darkness always comes too soon
Yet so full of life and goodness is my ball
I cannot help but heed its call
My ball cries out for truth and peace
In hope that this madness will cease
My ball is strong, and yet so weak
With words, I wish my ball could speak
And say to you as it does to me
This ball is not a toy you see

FRIENDS

Sorry, I don't feel towards you
The way you'd like me to
But, believe me, sugar
I really didn't mean to hurt you
Now there's nothing I can do
To help you get over the pain
And no matter how hard we try
Things will never be the same
How it all happened
It's so hard for me to understand
All I know is that tonight
You asked me for my hand
And when I told you "no"
It was all so plain to see
Our friendship was not
The same to you as it was to me
No matter what I say
I feel I bear the blame
For the feelings that we had
Will never be the same
You know I really feel sad
I think this is the end
Even though we said
We'd be each other's friend
Who knows what lie ahead
Maybe you'll get your wish
Until that time, my friend
On your cheek I plant a kiss

HOW LONG?

How long are they going to last?
The sun, the moon, the land
How long are they going to last?
These structures built by man
How long before the Earth
Vomits out all our trash?
How long before the towers
And the bridges begin to crash?
How long do you think we have
While Mother Nature provides for us?
How long do you think it'll be
Before she puts up a fuss?

INSANITY

You can call this what you like
I'll call it as I see it
Just because you think we have
What some may call a perfect fit
Is no reason to go on
When there is no you and me
It is going to rain pain
When we are hit by this Insanity

I'm really a little more
Concerned than maybe you are
But I think I have, for sure,
More reason than you by far
So please just try to feel me
I, too, must accept the blame
For being inside this Insanity

This situation is old
The decision must be made
We have to release our hold
As we watch everything fade
This is some strange destiny
Trying to keep us locked up
As prisoners of this Insanity

RUN OF THE MILL

Wake up child, a brand new day has just begun
More heartaches and anguish for you to face
Many challenges are waiting to be won
Though it is a bit early to end the race
And much too soon to start the prayer
Lord, what happiness when this day is done
You only ask that you can remain where
The earth refuses to hide from the sun

Everyone is after their piece of the pie
A virtue that never fails to blow my mind
As the day goes on ask yourself why
Are we caught inside such an ugly bind
In the midst it dawns on you
Though life still hasn't unraveled its pun
There's no need to cry, no need to be blue
The earth will always draw light from the sun

Everyday trials can make you so tense
That it becomes hard just to be you
And sometimes nothing makes any sense
But you keep going cause life isn't through
In your journey to reach many of your goals
You find that it is not always fun
To be one among many of the helpless souls
Watching the earth as it chases the sun

THE FIRST SNOW

The first snow came like dust from an angel's wings

Like feathers from a dove and other beautiful things

Like miniature cotton balls gently floating down

Swallowing the filthy things as it kissed the ground

It came and covered just about everything

Giving us a chance for a fresher spring

Like floating pearls blowing in the wind

Like diamond studs earth's starlight kin

The first snow came like dust from an angel's wings

Like feathers from a dove and other beautiful things

BLESSING

I was kind of down this morning

Then I saw your face

I said a "Te Ja" prayer

For God had shown me grace

I was down and under today

Then you smiled at me

I thought that you were sent

By heaven so especially

I was kind of blue this evening

You gave me a possibility

I thanked the Lord above

For this blessing sent to me

FOOL'S GAME

It seems that man has made us out of a fool

While we were thinking that we were so cool

He instilled in us everything wrong

And didn't teach us a thing in school

Right under our noses they have cheated us

Made our hearts drop and our souls play in dust

We were set up to fight one another

So we lost our faith as well as our trust

Life, sometimes, can truly be a fool's game

It seems that we are living it in vain

We 've lost so much of who we truly are

That we even blame the Lord's holy name

BEST WISHES

Be bold and brave and yet be fearful

For the roads in life will surely be tearful

Be clever and wise and yet be mute

The rivalry around will cause dispute

Be tough and strong, and yet be weak

For the answers in wisdom is what you seek

Be alert and unafraid to speak you mind

But also know where silence you may find

The road to success is long and dreary

Do not for a moment let your faith grow weary

Stick steadily on course with only the fact

For only with trust and honesty can you relax

The greatest test of life is to endure

For with perseverance the reward is sure

Enjoy your life, may your dreams come true

Best wishes is what this poem brings to you.

APPRECIATION

Sometimes, at night, I stare up at my cloudy bed

And I see the lights that cluster around my head

I think of the stars, planets and the Milky Way

Thank God for such a lovely night is what I pray

At dawn, I wake up to see the sun's fiery blaze

I can admire its beauty, even in my sleepy daze

I am so thankful and blessed to enjoy this day

Thank the Lord for this light is what I say

Thank you for the moonbeams as a guide in the night

Thank you for the sunbeams with its glorious light

Thank you for the nights and also for the days

Thanks so very much to You be all my praise

FUN HOUSE

All passengers please get in
The journey is about to begin
This ride is free; hence
You must bear the consequence
Round and around it goes
Where it leads you, nobody knows
Crashing through steel gate doors
To a street with junkies and whores
Drunken fools stumble toward you
Politicians sit at tables to argue
Teachers strike when school bells ring
Young folks are always doing their thing
Uprisers are talking about revolution
Scientists in a lab trying to prove evolution
The royals are sipping tea in the den
Preachers in a sanctuary saying ""Amen"
Alcoholic drinking their poison in a bar
Racers driving the Daytona 500 in their car
Riots, rapes, shooting out
The story is the same all about
The chase continues on and on
Soon we all will be dead and gone
Life if lost and love is strange
God is true but things must change
A man works hard both day and night
To see his family die is an ugly sight
Is this what life should truly be
Is this the life for you and me
Life can really be such a louse
If we keep living in the Fun House

THE BOND

Though we may not always be on the same page
Perhaps because our feelings, we could not gauge
We are in the same chapter of the same book
Despite of the many different paths we took

It's definitely not about me and it's not about you
It is about "us" and you know that is true
Our love is a constant yet changing stream
Our role is sure, no way is this a dream

It seems we were always having a major fight
I came from the left and you came from the right
We're centered now so no one else will ever do
Reciprocally, it's you for me and me for you

Even when there is sometimes a need to be free
I realize this is where I need to be
Making it alone is easy if I try
But together we can watch our children fly

Whenever I look into our children's eyes
I know this bond can't be easily untied
The bond we have is so strong and it is real
That bond is tough nothing can break its seal

EVERLASTING

Let the love which we possess
Be the cause of our happiness
Let this love that fills my heart
Keep us close even when we're apart

Let the star twinkling in my eye
Grow ever bright and never die
Let the smile that lights up my face
Be filled with joy when we embrace

Let the sweet song which fills my ears
Never fade and last throughout our years
Let the feelings that run through me
Stay true and never cease to be

Let all the thoughts that roam my mind
Remain sweet, soft, tender and kind
Let the pride that swells my soul
Be the pride that never grows old

Let all the beauty that I see
Remind me of you and you of me
Let the love I have for you
Last forever until time is through

ADELA GIBSON

LOVE'S LETTER

Dear Love,

I do believe in you
Because you gave me the reason
To love you in any season

You know that I am not a toy
Not an occasional treasure
I am every moment's pleasure

I see the rainbows of my life
It is the gift of your love's light
That makes my smile so wide and bright

My destiny will follow yours
From the place where our love began
To the place where the rainbow ends

I am so in love with you
You are so beautiful to me
Therefore, I am

Sincerely Yours

DID YOU EVER? II

Did you ever reach down
Into the center of yourself
Deep down into the core
Into the eye of yourself
And pulled hard until
It showed on the outside

Did you take a good look
At it, it being you
You, the ruler of your destiny
Did you turn the insides out
And look deeply until you saw
Clearly your true colors

Did colors blind you
Or did they mingle softly
With the stars in the universe
Which you also are part of
Did you understand what you saw
And did you like it?

THE DARK

Alone I wander in the dark
Through the swamps and through the meadows
Perceiving which way I should go
To learn the secret of shadows

I lay me down inside the dark
Things around me make me wonder
But no longer am I afraid
Of the dark I've now grown fonder

The dark is now an open book
Now that I know what to look for
I see the answers right ahead
Life is much clearer than before

I will continue in the dark
So I'll be ready for the light
Just like inside my mother's womb
I didn't know day; I didn't know night

But yet, in the dark I was safe
Away from the dangers of earth
Safe from the tragedies of life
Until the sacred day of birth

And then return into the dark
Once I've taken my final breath
Then into the radiant light
Along the pathway of my death

THE POSITIVE

The spirit of success
Is surely to know
When to take action
And when to let go.

The spirit of wisdom
Is to know the sign
Of that which was lost
But now we can find.

The spirit of our love
Is for all to see
Loving each other
Will set us all free.

RAIN BALLERINAS

Gently, softly with much grace and such flair
From saturated clouds they "pirouette"
Whirling, twirling and spinning in the air
Briskly they plop, passé and "plié"

They have so much fun and also power
It is awesome to watch them float around
On a tree leaf or inside a flower
You can see their joy as they hit the ground

They jump so high they almost seem to fly
In tutus of soft silvery sequin
They lift their arms reaching toward the sky
While the earth waits with her arms wide open

The skies clap with their thunderous delight
As all the rainbows and the clouds unfurl
They take their bows in brightly flashing light
They're the rain ballerinas of the world

DREAM

Last night I dreamed that I saw you
We ran toward each other
Our arms outstretched, tears streaming
In slow motion, it had been ... so long

Last night I dreamed you were here
There was love all around us
The stars were bright, the music soft
Happy because paradise ... had come

Last night I dreamed I kissed you
Eyes closed, hearts beating wildly
 Angels sang about our joy
Time is now for this dream to ... come true

IF ONLY

If only love could always win
We'd love forever and again
Till time passes its final year
Our love would always be right here

If only love could always win
We'd have loved ever since Eden
Until we're in Revelation
Our love needs no contemplation

If only love could always win
We'd be each other's synonym
Forming the most perfect haiku
That clearly defines me and you

If only love could always win
We'd love forever and again
Till the stars fade into the sun
You and I would always be one

GEORGIE PORGIE

Georgie Porgie, pudding and pie
Kissed my cheek and made me cry
All my dreams have faded away
And Georgie won't come out to play

Georgie, I said, please tell me why
All he could say to me was "Bye"
I didn't plead, I couldn't beg
Even though this was love's last leg

Georgie, I said, you are too cruel
He said, Hey, girl I am no fool
He said I love you can't you see
But it's not time for you and me

That's Georgie -- all pudding and pie
He kissed my lips then made me cry
Georgie, why did you go away
Please, Georgie, please come out today

PASSION

Somewhere from deep within
My eyes reflected the image of you
Where the sparkle in your eyes mirrors mine

Somehow your love's strength
Is the one true and failsafe remedy
For my own ability to be strong

Some place where love reigns
Our togetherness will be understood
In its regal joy and intensity

Something in your eyes
Ignites our love like a crimson sunrise
Against the smooth black coal of our passion

RAINBOW

Wanted to sketch a picture of words
For you, about you

Wanted to put an accent on
Your smile, your glow

Wanted you to see your colours
As I do – a rainbow

AQUAPHOBIA

We stood at opposite sides of an ocean
Neither wanting to be first to test the water
You, waiting for me, -- me afraid
Both trying to get clues from a shoreline view
Without the effect of kaleidoscopic mistiness
Maybe finding the oasis really isn't there
That it is all a part a desert mirage
With waves growling their aggravation
Like a rippling serenade of bursting bubbles
Or getting lost inside the magical tides
And finding treasures buried down deep
Reflecting of our inner free-flowing voice
A dream with colors too vivid for consideration
We can touch it to see if it is real
There is fear we may drown inside this dream
But the fear of not knowing is even greater

MY LIGHT

Who are You?
Who loves me ever so deeply
And strokes my face within the sun
Who is a friend when life is crude
And lets me rest when it is done

Who are You?
Who sets the path for me to follow
And guides me when I am wrong
Who raises me above the storm
And is the one who keeps me strong

Who are You?
Who makes my bed from velvet skies
And remembers me during strife
Who makes my rivers flow so even
And sails with me, the seas of life

Who are You?
Who many call by many names
And yet there is but only One
Who loves the most in all the world
Without your love there just is none!

Just When I Was Sure

Just when I was sure that I had forgot
I started to think about you a lot
All the memories sent my head reeling
Then suddenly I had this strange feeling
I knew at once, I had to have you back
I knew for certain, you are what I lack
I really want to feel what I felt before
Tell me, is it real, I need to be sure
There's a place in my heart that's just for you
You know just like I do that this is true
You have the special key it's yours alone
We have what it takes to make it our own
To some, this must sound a little crazy
But certainly there's nothing wrong with me
Except I was sure that I had forgot
Now I am thinking about you a lot

WRITE FOR ME

Come on baby, I want to feel you sing
Come on now sugar let's do our thing
I know things aren't what they used to be
But please won't you do your dance for me
Write for me, one time, now don't be shy
I know you can, you've just got to try
Just make the words appear like magic
Not doing this now would be tragic
It feels so good after all this time
Let's do it again, just one more rhyme
We have got the right kind of weather
So we can keep it all together
And say the things we needed to say
And here finally it is our day
It is all up to you to tell me when
We will bring this poem to an end

DECEMBER SONG

I want this December song
To be filled with joy until the end
Each note ecstatic on its own
Sweet December sing along

I hope that this month of cheer
Will be bubbling with much happiness
Throughout and right over into
The bright new and coming year

I pray this December kiss
Will bring us some euphoric treasures
Filled with everlasting gladness
That our love truly exists

LIFE MUSIC

Life is the middle C on a musical staff
Where the notes come together and meet
To form their melody oh so sweet

The sharps and flats work together
Composing life's definitive melody
Keeping the tempo flowing so free

The clefs along with the notes
Set up the specific guideline
That lead to harmony so divine

Life is the middle C on a musical staff
Where the notes come together and meet
To form their melody oh so sweet

Sometimes crescendo at other times allegro
With choruses spun out in four quarter time
Singing each note in perfect rhyme

The song of life can be clear and sweet
Each rest defining the tune
As soft as the month of June

Life is the middle C on a musical staff
Where the notes come together and meet
To form their melody of life so sweet

HAUNTED

Shadowy pasts keep haunting me
Yesteryears that don't born the morrow
Remind me of the glee
And at the same time the sorrow

My today is bright and shining
It bears promise of the future's treasure
But yesterday's hope is still there whining
In the background of this new found pleasure

Release me please so I that I may be
Free from the passionate caress of gloom
You have no hold or chains on me
Old seedlings will no longer give bloom

Spring forth the new, lead the old away
For they belong on the wings of the past
And should not mingle with the new day
But to undo what wicked spells were cast

JACK AND JILL

Jack and Jill went up the hill
They were searching for a dream
The roads were too cramped for them
And now they're not a team

Up at the top of the hill
They met people of the real world
Who simply have no time
For a foolish boy and girl

In a world where hate prevails
And love is an abandoned child
There's very little you can do
To get away from what is wild

If you have good – it can go bad
Or it will be taken away
Jealousy is the sure motive
When they act like devils at play

All that is left are some memories
Of innocent love left to die
For now that Jack is gray and old
Jill's no longer little and shy

Jack and Jill, may have gone too far
Cause they never made it back down the hill
They got lost looking for the dream
They'd really wanted to fulfill

EMPTINESS

Empty heart, empty hand
No love, no man
Cold nights, cold bed
May as well be dead
No sugar No honey
Life is not funny
Can't give, can't take
Not even for goodness sake
Empty heart, empty hand
Nobody gives a damn

MI TIA JUANA

Mi Tia Juana
Es como mi hermana

A little lady with a big heart
And a smile to match

Apprendido mucho
baja her loving watch

Le gustaban las flores
Especialmente las morning glories

We watched them close
En la noche

Entonces se abriria
again the very next day

I learned to appreciate
The miracles of the earth

And to marvel at all that
Gives life its worth

Mi Tia Juana
Es como mi Hermana

Little lady with a big heart
And a matching smile

Mi Tia Juana
Es como mi Hermana

Sharing love in her
Own sweet style

LOVING

If he wanted me to kiss him
Wouldn't my bosom swell with emotions
Which words could never explain

And wouldn't I sing him a serenade
Inside his mouth that only he can hear
And wouldn't we kiss lovingly

If he wanted me to love him
Wouldn't I surround his being
With my mellow sweet softness

And wouldn't the music of our breath
Slowly subside and drift into ecstasy
Bringing back the lovely dawn

Spiritual Manna

Here I am in peaceful, loving solitude

Offering much earnest and heartfelt gratitude

For all that was, all that is and will ever be

Knowing life is so much more than we can see

THE RAINBOW'S END

I stuck my hand deep down and scraped the pot
My hands were bleeding, it was much too hot
I pulled my hand out, held it to my lips
It hurt me so bad, my poor fingertips

I kissed them softly, so there'd be no pain
I spread them out slow and closed them again
I watched as they healed and saw them grow strong
With the help of Source, it will not take long

Again in the pot, taking time and care
Not moving fast or disturbing a hair
The bottom was smooth, I felt there was love
It filled me with joy that came from above

I knew that this time, there was not a doubt
That love was for me, I needed to shout
And scream to the hills which don't understand
That inside this pot lays pure golden sand

Holding the glow of angels and their light
Keeping our fire hot and burning bright
So we can see when the curtain's pulled back
That the light has no deficit or lack

PATHWAYS

When we fly high
We really soar
We cannot lie
We want some more

When we are down
We drag our tail
Along the ground
That's how we fail

It gets so bad
When we go deep
We get so mad
It makes us weep

Then we forget
The promise made
To never let
The good word fade

We spread our wings
To fly again
Over the springs
And through the rain

Then we fly high
And touch the sun
Up in the sky
Just having fun

CONFIDENCE

Life starts with a lot of fun and games
Sometimes it ends with some dirty names
I am not in search of lost glory
I just want to tell the true story

There's a dark place far across the track
Somewhere that we should never go back
Your dad and mine went to similar schools
How is that only one get good tools

Your mom climbed all the way to the top
My mom was there too but had to stop
My dad was searched for things he never had
Your dad had it all and was very glad

Things are evolving, I thank God for that
Maybe someday my wallet will get fat
And I can walk without the threat of frisk
To lose the label of "person at risk"

I am getting old and a little gray
With help I can thankfully find my way
So please don't put my time spent asunder
I can help you get from deep down under

There is still a very long way to go
Don't listen to those who always say "no"
Always follow your heart and stay on track
And don't you ever, no never, look back

Whatever you do, hold faith very tight
Let it lead you into your sacred light
Keep right on going and do not give up
Stop only when you have the winner's cup

This life is just a temporary host
Changing when it's time to give up the ghost
Then we can see what life is all about
Only then will there be no fear or doubt

THE LOVE THAT TRULY MATTERS

Its hard to grow without love and kisses
They are the first on my list of wishes
My dreams showed me the life I was to live
And to accept the love I had to give

Right now this is what I want to create
I want to seed roots and proliferate
Being mindful of the things I pray for
Helps them sprout quickly and grow even more

Just when you think anguish has taken hold
You become part of the best story told
Your story can have a solid ending
If you're sure at the very beginning

Just specify what you want when you speak
Only then will you achieve what you seek
This is a fate that has been tried and true
The love that matters is inside of you